SAMUEL BARBER

MUSIC FOR SOPRANO
AND ORCHESTRA

Operatic and Concert Scenes

REDUCTION FOR VOICE AND PIANO

G. SCHIRMER, Inc.

DISTRIBUTED BY

HAL•LEONARD®
CORPORATION
7777 W. BLUEMOUND RD. P.O. BOX 13819 MILWAUKEE, WI 53213

Orchestral parts for all selections contained in this
collection are available on rental from the publisher.

RECORDINGS

Knoxville: Summer of 1915
    Columbia ML5843. Eleanor Steber, soloist; Dumbarton Oaks
    Chamber Orchestra, William Strickland, conductor.

Vanessa
    RCA Victor LM6138/LS6138: Metropolitan Opera, Dimitri
    Mitropoulos, conductor.

  Do not utter a word
    RCA Victor LM2898/LS2898 Prima Donna, Vol. I; Leontyne Price

Andromache's Farewell
    CBS ML5912/MS6512: Martina Arroyo, soloist; New York
    Philharmonic, Thomas Schippers, conductor.

CONTENTS

KNOXVILLE: SUMMER OF 1915

Duration: approximately 16 minutes

This work was first performed by Eleanor Steber with the Boston Symphony Orchestra under the direction of Serge Koussevitzky on April 9, 1948. It is recorded on Columbia ML 5843 by Miss Steber and the Dumbarton Oaks Chamber Orchestra, conducted by William Strickland.

We are talking now of summer evenings in Knoxville Tennessee in the time that I lived there so successfully disguised to myself as a child.

. . . It has become that time of evening when people sit on their porches, rocking gently and talking gently and watching the street and the standing up into their sphere of possession of the trees, of birds' hung havens, hangars. People go by; things go by. A horse, drawing a buggy, breaking his hollow iron music on the asphalt: a loud auto: a quiet auto: people in pairs, not in a hurry, scuffling, switching their weight of aestival body, talking casually, the taste hovering over them of vanilla, strawberry, pasteboard, and starched milk, the image upon them of lovers and horsemen, squared with clowns in hueless amber.

A streetcar raising its iron moan; stopping; belling and starting, stertorous; rousing and raising again its iron increasing moan and swimming its gold windows and straw seats on past and past and past, the bleak spark crackling and cursing above it like a small malignant spirit set to dog its tracks; the iron whine rises on rising speed; still risen, faints; halts; the faint stinging bell; rises again, still fainter; fainting, lifting, lifts, faints foregone: forgotten. Now is the night one blue dew.

> Now is the night one blue dew, my father has drained, he has coiled the hose.
>
> Low on the length of lawns, a frailing of fire who breathes . . .
>
> Parents on porches: rock and rock. From damp strings morning glories hang their ancient faces.
>
> The dry and exalted noise of the locusts from all the air at once enchants my eardrums.

On the rough wet grass of the back yard my father and mother have spread quilts. We all lie there, my mother, my father, my uncle, my aunt, and I too am lying there . . . They are not talking much, and the talk is quiet, of nothing in particular, of nothing at all in particular, of nothing at all. The stars are wide and alive, they seem each like a smile of great sweetness, and they seem very near. All my people are larger bodies than mine, . . . with voices gentle and meaningless like the voices of sleeping birds. One is an artist, he is living at home. One is a musician, she is living at home. One is my mother who is good to me. One is my father who is good to me . . . By some chance, here they are, all on this earth; and who shall ever tell the sorrow of being on this earth, lying, on quilts, on the grass, in a summer evening, among the sounds of the night . . . May God bless my people, my uncle, my aunt, my mother, my good father, oh, remember them kindly in their time of trouble; and in the hour of their taking away.

After a little I am taken in and put to bed. Sleep, soft smiling, draws me unto her: and those receive me, who quietly treat me, as one familiar and well-beloved in that home: but will not, oh, will not, not now, not ever; but will not ever tell me who I am.

JAMES AGEE

In memory of my Father

Knoxville: Summer of 1915

For Voice and Orchestra

James Agee*

Samuel Barber, Op.24
Reduction for Piano by the Composer

"We are talking now of summer evenings in Knoxville Tennessee in the time that I lived there so
successfully disguised to myself as a child."

*Words used by permission of James Agee and *Partisan Review*.

rock - ing gen - tly and talk - ing gen - tly   and watch-ing the street and the

sempre legato

stand - ing up in-to their sphere of pos - ses - sion___ of the trees, of birds' hung

Str.

espr.

ha - vens,___ hang - ars.___

Fl.

Strs.

Peo-ple go by; things go by.   A horse, draw-ing a bug-gy,

Cl.

breaking his hollow iron music on the asphalt: a loud auto; a quiet auto: people in pairs, not in a hurry, scuffling switching their weight of aestival body, talking casually,— the taste hov-'ring over them of vanilla,

straw-ber-ry, paste-board, and starched milk, the

im-age up-on them of lov - ers and horse-men, squared with clowns ___ in

hue - less am - - ber.

Low on the length of lawns_____ a frail-ing of fire_____ who

breathes._____ Par-ents on porch-es; rock and rock.

From damp strings morn-ing-glo-ries__ hang their an-cient

fa - ces. The dry and ex - alt - ed

noise of the lo-custs ___ from all the air _____ at __ once _____ en-

chants my ear - drums.

On the rough wet grass of the back-yard my fa - ther and moth-er have spread quilts.___ We all lie there, my moth - er, my fa - ther, my un - cle, my aunt,___ and I too am ly - ing there.___

They are not talk-ing much, and the talk is qui - et, of noth-ing _ in par-

senza Ped.

tic - u - lar, _ of noth-ing at all in par-

tic - u - lar, _ of noth-ing at all. The

stars are wide and a - live, they seem _

each like a smile of great sweet - ness,

and they seem ver - y near. All my peo - ple are

lar - ger bod - ies __ than mine, __

with voic - es gen - tle and mean - ing-less like the voic - es of

sleep - ing birds._____ One is an art - ist, he is

liv - ing at home. One is a mu - si - cian, she is

liv - ing at home. One is my moth - er who is

good to me. One is my fa - ther who is

on the grass, _____ in a sum-mer eve - ning,

a-mong the sounds of the night. _____

22 **Meno mosso** ♩ = 72 *mp with intensity and deep feeling*

May God _____ bless ___ my

peo - ple, my un - cle, my aunt, my moth - er, my good fa - ther,

oh, re-mem-ber them kind-ly in their time of trou-ble;

moving ahead

and in the hour_____ of their ta-king a-

broadly

way.

full Brass
molto espressivo

Tutti

mar-

will not ev - er tell me who I am.

THREE SCENES
FROM "VANESSA"

Do not utter a word
Duration: 4'30"

Must the winter come so soon?
Duration: 2'

Under the willow tree
Duration: 2'15"

Vanessa had its first performance on January 15, 1958 at the Metropolitan Opera House in New York. The production was staged by Gian Carlo Menotti and conducted by Dimitri Mitropoulos. It is recorded on Columbia LM/LSC 6138 with Eleanor Steber, Nicolai Gedda, Rosalind Elias and the Metropolitan Opera Company, conducted by Dimitri Mitropoulos.

Do not utter a word

from the opera "Vanessa"

Gian Carlo Menotti

Samuel Barber, Op. 32

For o-ver twen - ty years _____ in still-ness, in si-lence,

poco rall. *a tempo*

I have wait-ed for you. _____ I have al-ways been

sure, I have al-ways known you would come back to me, An - a-tol; _ I have scarce-ly

breathed so that Life should not leave its trace and that noth-ing might change in me_

for___ you.___

ff appassionato

f

f
Now lis - ten,_____

p

allarg. molto   *mf*   *a tempo*

lis - ten,_
lis - ten well:_____

allarg. molto   *a tempo*

f

be-gins__ when Love__ has died,_____ when Love has died.

Tell me, An-a-tol,____ do you love me? Do you still

love me as once you did?____ For if you do not, I shall

ask you to leave my house this ver-y night!_____

Must the winter come so soon?

from the opera "Vanessa"

for Mezzo-Soprano

Gian Carlo Menotti

Samuel Barber

Must the win-ter come so soon?

Night aft-er night I

hear the hun-gry deer wan-der weep-ing in the woods,

*⌐▬ = triplet throughout

and_from his house of brit-tle bark_ hoots_ the fro - zen owl.

Must the win-ter come so soon?

Here_____ in this for - est nei-ther dawn nor sun - set

marks the pas-sing of the days._____

It is a long win-ter here.

Must the win-ter__ come so soon?_____

Under the Willow Tree

from the opera "Vanessa"

Duet

Gian Carlo Menotti

Samuel Barber

doves cry, ah ____ oh! Where shall we sleep, my love, whith - er

shall we fly? Where shall we sleep, my love, whith - er shall we fly? ____

The wood has swal - lowed the moon, the fog has swal -

_ lowed the shore, the green toad has _ swal-lowed the key to my door.

ANDROMACHE'S FAREWELL

Duration: 12 minutes

This work was commissioned by the New York Philharmonic in cele-
bration of its opening season in Lincoln Center for the Performing Arts,
and first performed on April 4,1963 by Martina Arroyo, Thomas Schippers
conducting. It is recorded on Columbia ML5912, MS6512 by the same
artists.

Scene: an open space before Troy, which has just been captured by the Greeks. All Trojan men have been killed or have fled and the women and children are held captives. Each Trojan woman has been allotted to a Greek warrior and the ships are now ready to take them into exile. Andromache, widow of Hector, Prince of Troy, has been given as a slave-wife to the son of Achilles. She has just been told that she cannot take her little son with her in the ship. For it has been decreed by the Greeks that a hero's son must not be allowed to live and that he is to be hurled over the battlements of Troy. She bids him farewell. In the background the city is slowly burning. It is just before dawn.

The text is from "The Trojan Women" by Euripides, especially translated by John Patrick Creagh.

So you must die, my son,
my best-beloved, my own,
by savage hands and leave
your Mother comfortless.
Hector's valiant spirit, shield of thousands,
Is death to his own son.

My wedding day! it was my sorrow
that day I came to Hector's house
to bear my son. He was to be
Lord of all Asia and not for Greeks to slaughter.

My boy, you are weeping.
Do you know then what awaits you?
Why do you hold me so?
clutch at my dress? (a small bird
seeking shelter under my wing.)
Hector cannot come back
with his brave spear to save you.
He cannot come from the grave
nor any of his princes.

Instead, from the height, flung down! oh pitiless!
head foremost! falling! falling! . . . .
Thus will your life end.

Oh dearest embrace, sweet breathing of your body,
Was it for nothing that I nursed you, that I suffered?
consumed my heart with cares, all for nothing?

Now, and never again, kiss your Mother.
Come close, embrace me, who gave you life.
Put your arms around me, your mouth to mine . . . .
And then no more.

You Greeks, contrivers of such savagery.
Why must you kill this guiltless child?

Helen! you they call daughter of God,
I say you are the spawn of many fathers:
Malevolence, murder, hate, destruction—
all the evils that afflict the earth.
God curse you, Helen, for those eyes that brought
hideous carnage to the fair fields of Troy.

Take him then, take him away,
break his body on the rocks;
Cast him down, eat his flesh if that is your desire . . .
Now the Gods have destroyed us utterly,
And I can no longer
conceal my child from death. (*She relinquishes Astyanax.*)

Hide my head in shame;
Cast me in the ship,
as to that marriage bed
across the grave of my own son I come!

Andromache's Farewell

for Soprano and Orchestra

Samuel Barber, Op. 39

Allegro con fuoco ♩=100

Piano

allarg. poco a poco

rall. molto

(5) Moderato. with dignity ♩= 56

So_ you must die, my son, my best be - lov - ed, my own, by

sa - vage hands and leave your Moth - er com - fort - less._

Hec-tor's val-iant spir-it,____ shield__ of thou-sands, is death to his own son. _____

My wed-ding day! ____ It was my sor-row that

Andante un poco mosso ♩= 48

(with tenderness)

Oh dear-est em-brace,

sweet breath - ing of your bod - y, Was it for

(with hatred)

You Greeks,— con-triv-ers of such sav-age-ry,—

Why must you kill____ this guilt-less__ child?__

allarg.

⑯ Allegro molto ♩ = 108

Hel - en!__ Hel - en!__ You they_ call

Tempo I ♩ = 56
(She relinquishes Astyanax.)

pp

cresc. molto

ff

14

14

12

12

TWO SCENES FROM
"ANTHONY AND CLEOPATRA"

1. "Give me some music"
Duration: 7'45"

2. Death of Cleopatra
Duration: 8'

Antony and Cleopatra was commissioned by the Metropolitan Opera Association for the opening of the new Metropolitan Opera House in Lincoln Center, New York, on September 16, 1966.

1

We are in Egypt in Cleopatra's palace. Antony has left for Rome and there are rumors that he has married. The orchestral introduction portrays Cleopatra's fury when she demands the truth from a messenger and strikes him in her jealousy.

The music becomes more calm, recalling the tenderness of the lovers' separation. Bored, Cleopatra calls for music: "moody food of us that trade in love." She remembers how they first went fishing together when he called her "his serpent of old Nile." Her longing for him increases.

CLEOPATRA

Give me some music: music, moody
    food
Of us that trade in love . . . .
I'll none now!
Give me my angle, we'll to the river:
    there,
My music playing far off, I will betray
Tawny-finned fishes.
And as I draw them up,
I'll think them every one an Antony,
And say, "Ah,ha! y'are caught!"
That time — O times!
I laughed him out of patience; and that
    night
I laughed him into patience.
And the next morn ere the ninth hour
I drunk him to his bed:
Then put my crown and mantles on
    him,
While I wore his sword Philippan.
My man of men!
Charmian!
Give me to drink
    mandragora

That I might sleep out this great gap of
    time
My Antony is away.
My man of men!
O Charmian, where think'st that he is
    now?
Stands he, or sits he?
Or does he walk?
Or is he on his horse?
O happy horse, to bear the weight of
    Antony!
Do bravely, horse! for know'st thou
    whom thou movest?
The demi-Atlas of this earth.
He's speaking now, or murmuring:
"Where's my serpent of old Nile?"
(For so he calls me.)
Now I feed myself with most delicious
    poison.
Think on me,
That am with Phoebus' amorous pinches
    black,
And wrinkled deep in time . . .
Give me some music: music, moody
    food
Of us that trade in love.

2

Cleopatra has taken refuge in the pyramid after the defeat of her armies. Antony, who has stabbed himself, dies at her feet. The orchestra plays a funeral march as she decides to die with him. "Give me my robe, put on my crown," she commands and poisons herself by applying an asp which she has smuggled into the monument.

CLEOPATRA

Give me my robe, put on my crown, I
    have
Immortal longings in me. Now no more
The juice of Egypt's grape shall moist
    this lip.
Yare, yare, good Iras; quick, Methinks
    I hear
Antony call: I see him rouse himself
To praise my noble act.
Husband, I come:
Now to that name my courage prove my
    title!
I am fire, and air; my other elements
I give to baser life. So, have you done:
Come then, and take the last warmth
    of my lips.
Farewell, kind Charmian, Iras, long
    farewell.
Have I the aspic on my lips? Dost fall?
If thou and nature can so gently part,

The stroke of death is as a lover's pinch,
Which hurts, and is desired.
Come, thou mortal wretch.
(to an asp, which she applies to her
    breast)
With thy sharp teeth this knot intrin-
    sicate
Our life at once untie.
Peace, peace!
Dost thou not see my baby at my breast,
That sucks the nurse asleep?
As sweet as balm, as soft as air, as
    gentle —
O Antony! Nay, I will take thee too:
    (applying another asp to her arm)
What should I stay —
In this vile world?
Now I feed myself with most
    delicious poison
That I might sleep out
    this great gap of time.
My man of men!

1."Give me some music"

William Shakespeare   Samuel Barber, Op. 40

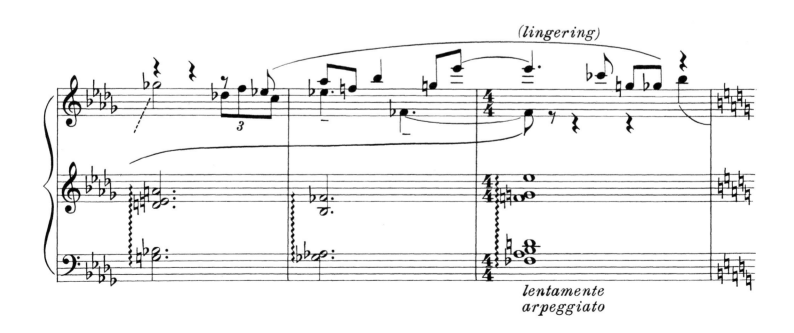

moving ahead slightly

Un poco allegro ♩=100

mp

simile

I'll none now!

Tempo I

♩=♪ (interrupting)

Give me my an-gle,___ we'll to the riv-er:___ there, My

mu-sic play-ing far off, _____ I will be-tray Taw-ny-finned fish-

- es. _____ And as I draw them up, _____

I'll think them ev-'ry one an An-to-ny, And say,_ "Ah, ha!

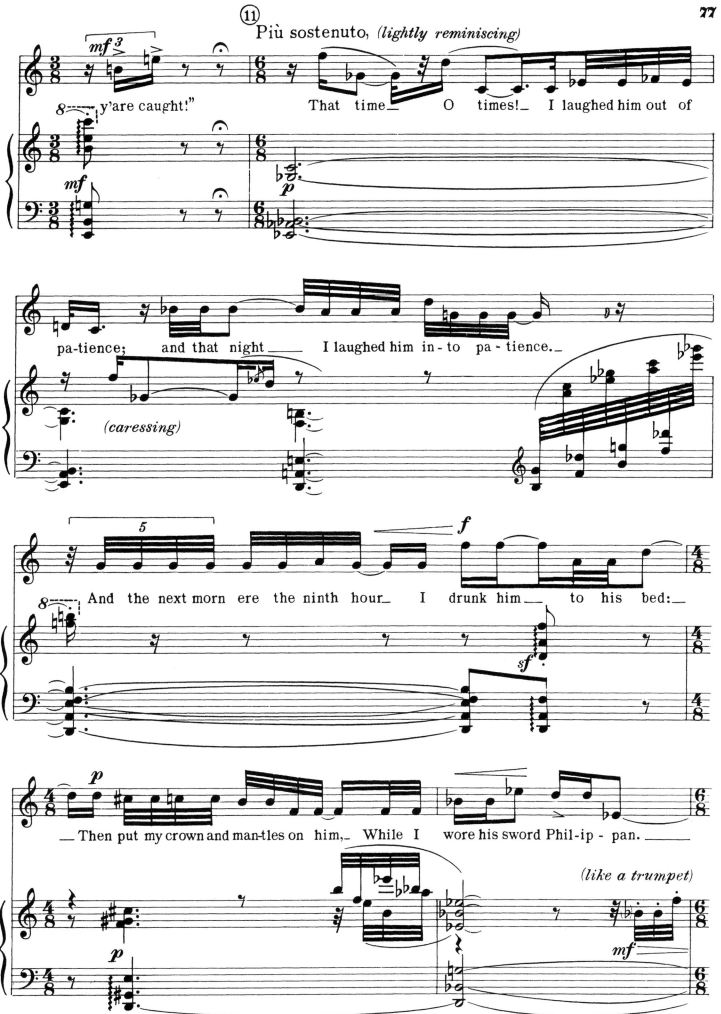

think'st that he is now? Stands he, or

espr.

sits he? Or does he walk?_____ Or is he on his horse?

(with constant motion)
mf

O hap- py horse, to bear the weight of An - to-

fp

so— he— calls ——— me.)

mp espr.

(16)

p (with increasing ardor and expansion)

Now ——————— I feed my-self — with most de-li-cious

(with pathos)

poi - son. Think on me,— That am with Phoe-bus' am'rous pinch-es

black, And wrin - kled deep in

duration 7' 45''

2. Death of Cleopatra

William Shakespeare

Samuel Barber, Op. 40

Andante maestoso, come una marcia ♩ = 56

Piano

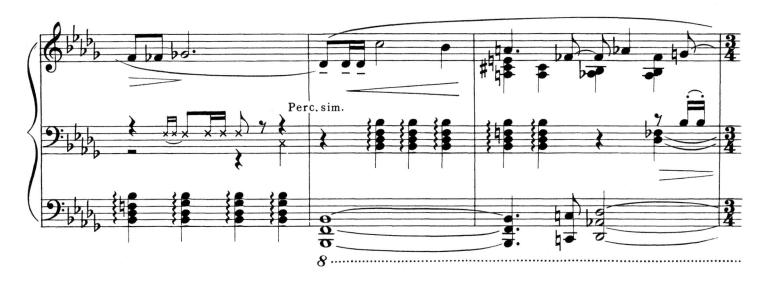

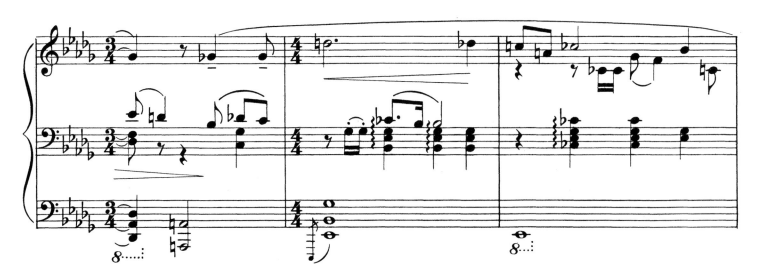

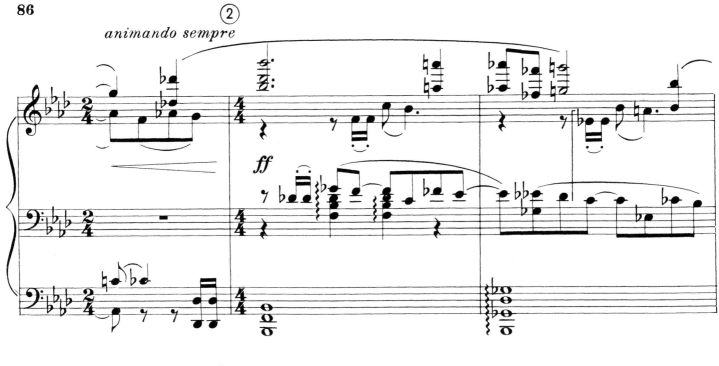

Cleopatra Tempo I

Give me my robe, put on my crown,— I have Im-mor-tal long-ings— in me.—

Now no more _____ The

juice of E - gypt's grape shall moist this lip.

Which hurts, and is de-sired.

(to an asp, which she applies to her breast)
⑧ Agitato, faster than before ♩ = 80

Come,____ thou mor-tal wretch.

mf (roughly, with biting accents)

With thy sharp teeth__ this knot in - trin - si - cate__ Our life at once un -

Peace, peace! Dost thou not see my ba - by at ___ my

breast,_____ That sucks the nurse a - sleep?___

As sweet as balm, as soft___ as air, as gen-tle...

O An - to - ny!___

(She applies another asp to her arm.)

Nay,— I will take thee, too:

What should I stay—

In this vile world?

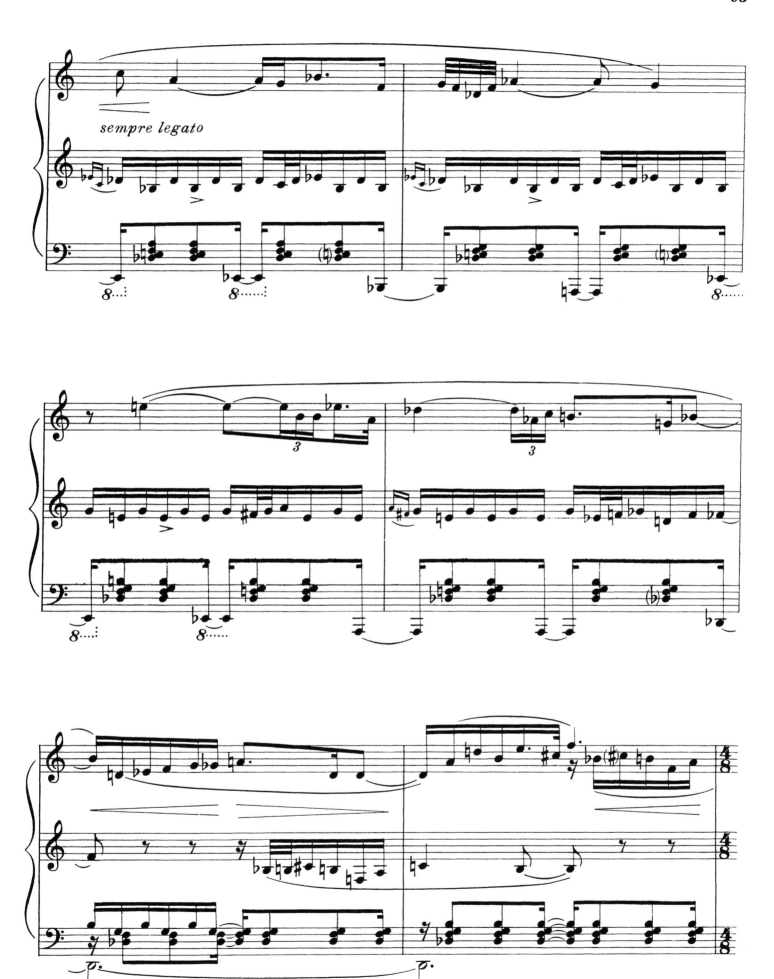

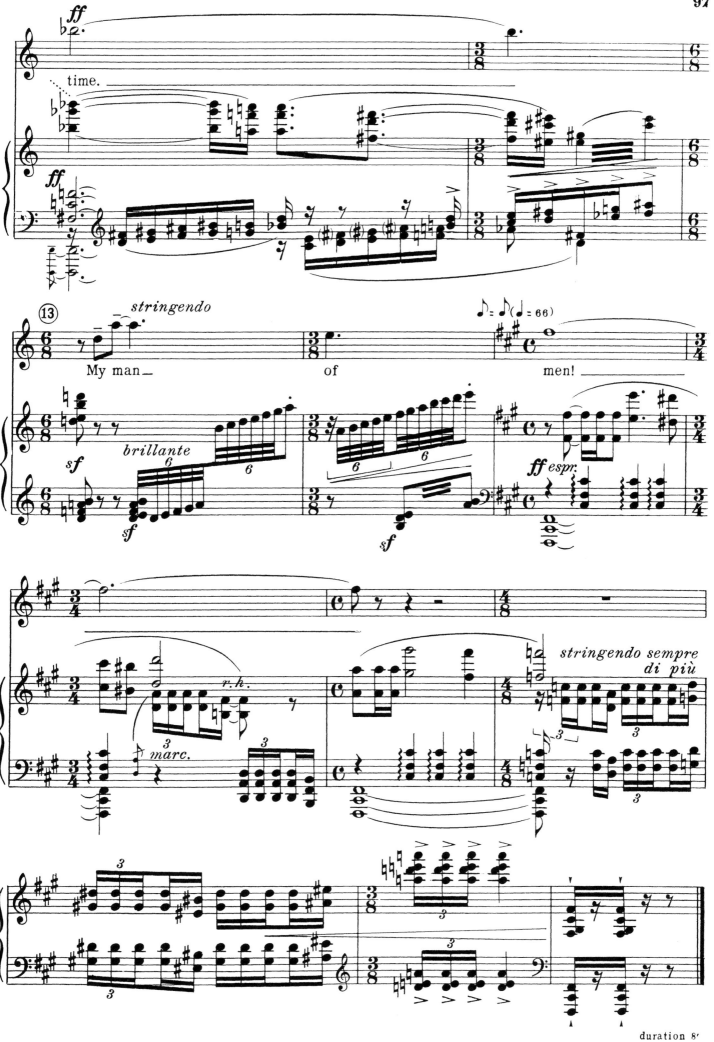

duration 8′